Learning to Write

Preparing for joined-up writing

GW00505914

Peter Smith

Age 4–6

Contents

Thomas Nelson and Sons Ltd
Nelson House Mayfield Road
Walton-on-Thames Surrey
KT12 5PL UK

51 York Place
Edinburgh
EH1 3JD UK

Thomas Nelson (Hong Kong) Ltd
Toppan Building 10/F
22a Westlands Road
Quarry Bay Hong Kong

Thomas Nelson Australia
102 Dodds Street
South Melbourne
Victoria 3205 Australia

Nelson Canada
1120 Birchmount Road
Scarborough Ontario
M1K 5G4 Canada

© Peter Smith 1993
Calligraphy by Annie Moring
Illustrations by Lynne Farmer and Paula L Cox

First published by Thomas Nelson and Sons Ltd exclusively for
W H Smith 1993

ISBN 0-17-424561-0
NPN 9 8 7 6 5 4 3 2 1

Printed in Hong Kong

Notes for parents

The aim
The aim of these two workbooks is to provide guidance and support for parents and children who want to work at home to improve children's handwriting. The *National Curriculum for English* includes the requirement that children begin to produce clear and legible joined-up writing by Level Three, which corresponds approximately to ages seven and eight. However, many schools begin teaching joined-up writing when children are much younger and these workbooks reflect that tendency.

The writing style
The *New Nelson Handwriting* style is taught in many schools. It is designed to be fluent and legible when written at different speeds. It is easy to learn and provides an excellent basis for the individual hand which each child is encouraged to develop at a later stage. The tasks in the two books are arranged sequentially, from learning the basic letter shapes to the point at which children become competent at joining. Letters are taught in 'families' depending on the way in which they are formed.

Posture and pencil grip
It helps children to write well if they sit comfortably at a table and chair. A right-hander needs to have the writing page in front of the right half of the body with a slight slope to the left. A left-hander should place the page in front of the left half of the body with a slight slope to the right. The pencil should be held lightly between the thumb and first two fingers, about 3-4 centimetres from the point.

The writing size
The models for learning and the spaces for practice are large, to ensure that children have room to make their letters and joins correctly.

Pencil control and patterns
Drawing, colouring and pattern making are included in the activities as they help develop fine motor skills in an enjoyable way. Some of the writing patterns are frequently practised because they relate to letter families. The swings pattern $\mathcal{UMU}$ is particularly important as it is the basis of most joins.

The joins
There are four kinds of join to be learned.

Join 1   Join 2   Join 3   Join 4

Fluency
The work in the two books should be done with care, but fluency is also important. Most units of pattern and groups of letters should be made with one continuous movement. Where letters require more than one movement, the directional arrows are numbered.

Using this book
Children can trace over the dotted or tinted lines before attempting freehand practice. The symbol • indicates the starting point.

indicates that the children are to write, and tells them to look carefully at the models, noting the starting points and directional arrows. These can be traced over with the blunt end of a pencil. Tracing paper can be used for extra practice.

Pages 1-7	develop fine motor control. Children will enjoy colouring in the shapes and this will also help the development of pencil control.
Pages 8-36	provide practice in letter and figure formation.
Page 37	provides an opportunity to compare print and joined writing through a humorous rhyme.
Pages 38-44	introduce joined writing with practice of the first two joins.

Patterns for pencil control
(ww)

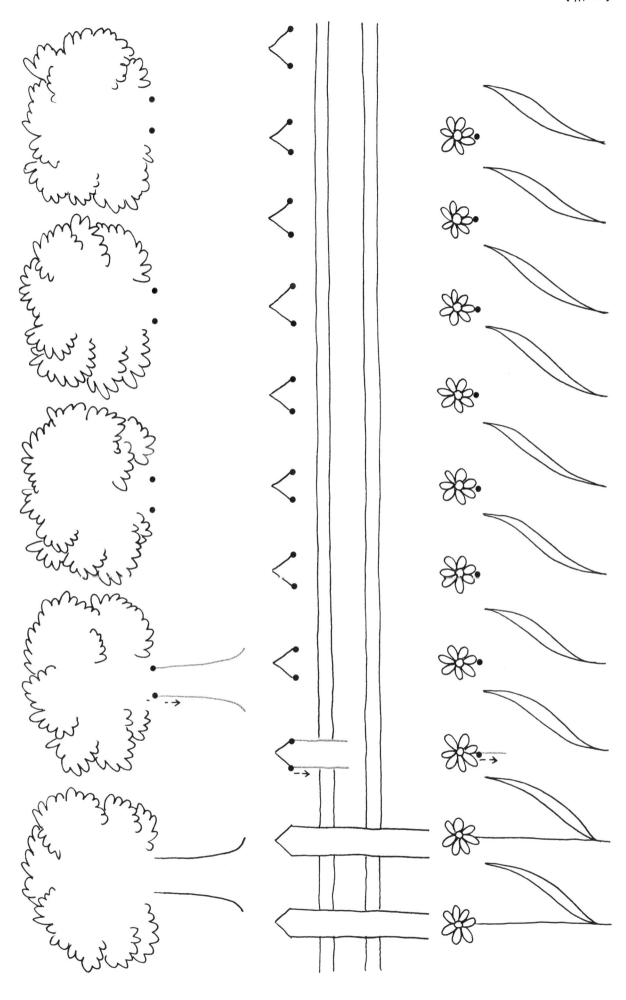

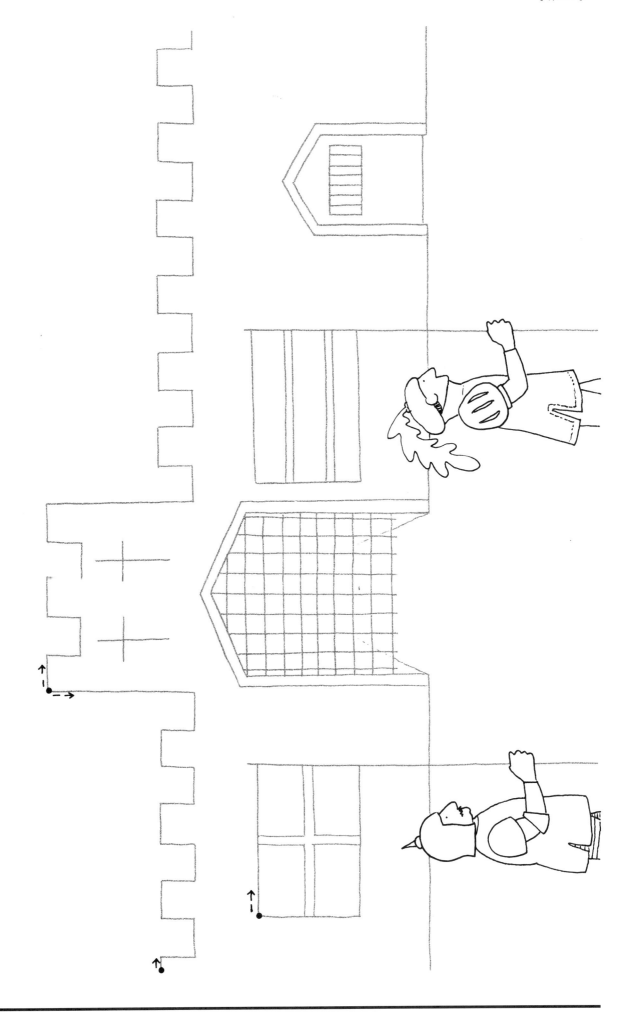

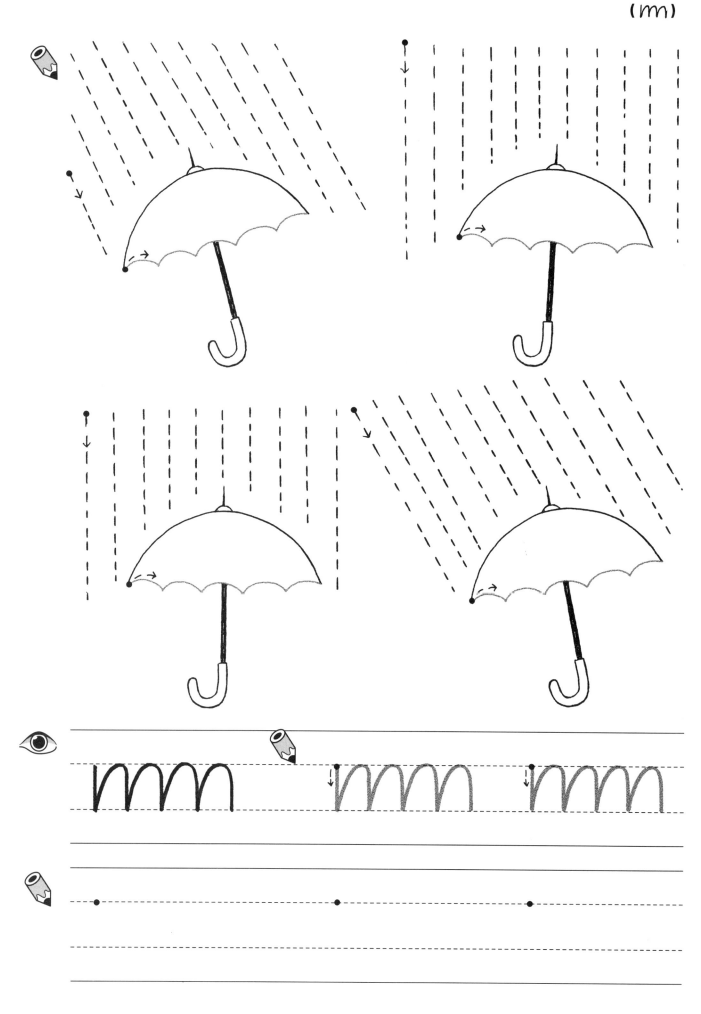

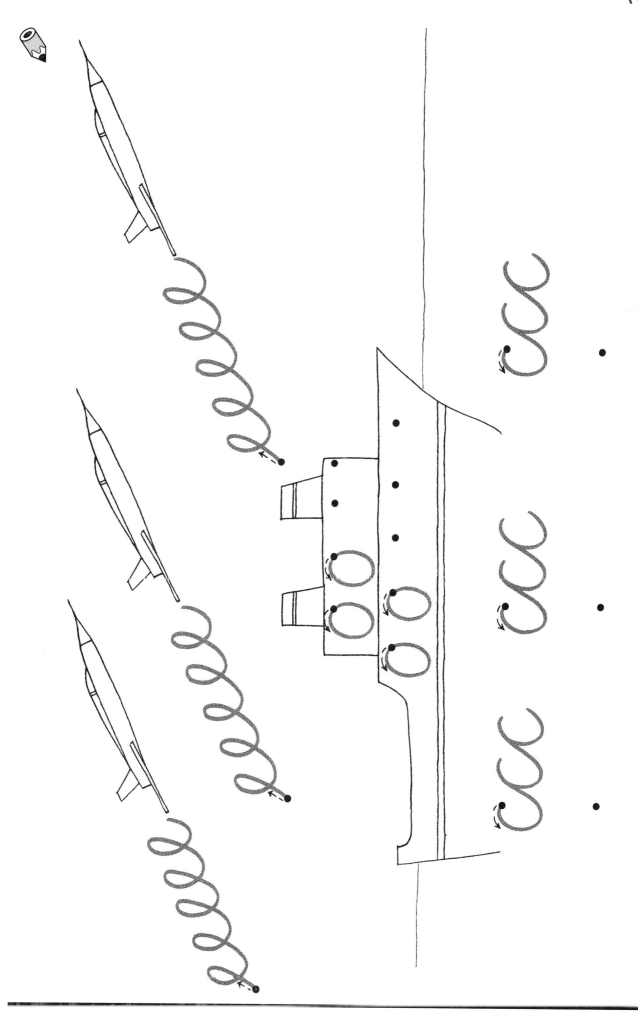

animals

cat

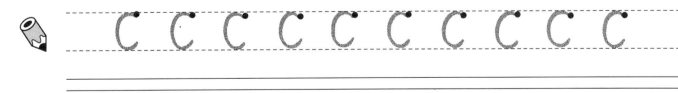

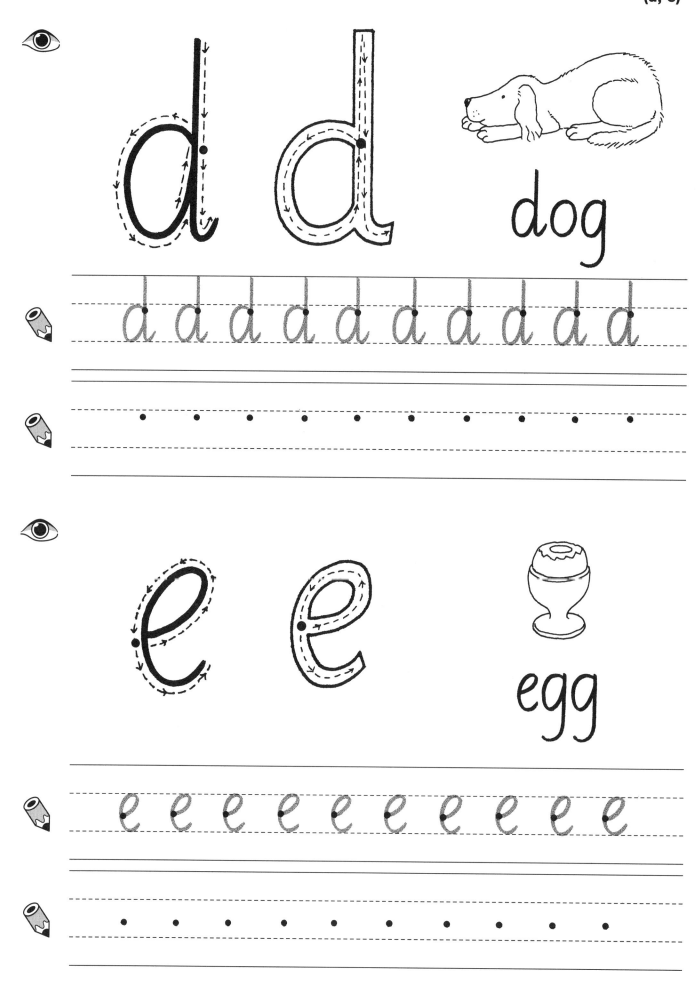

dog

egg

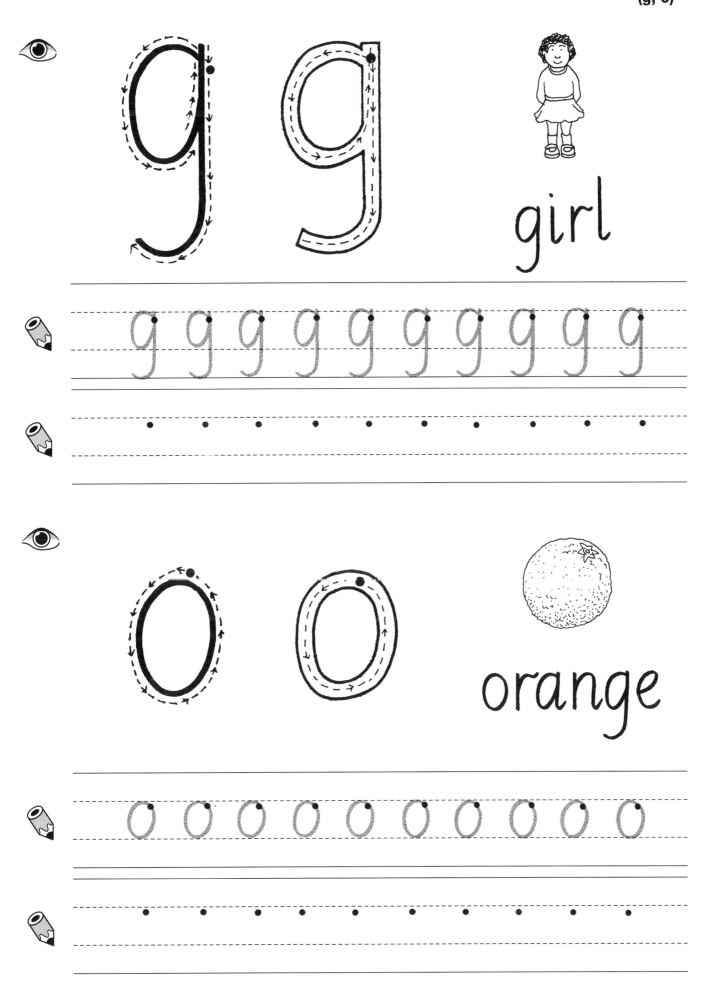

girl

orange

queen

bed

hat

king

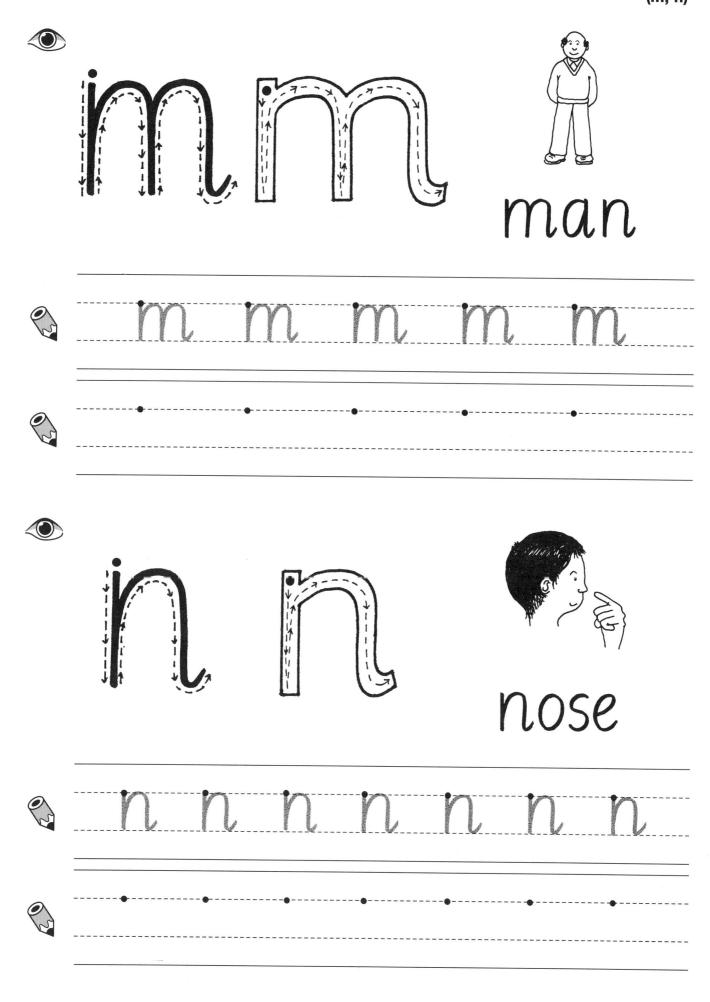

man

nose

pig

rabbit

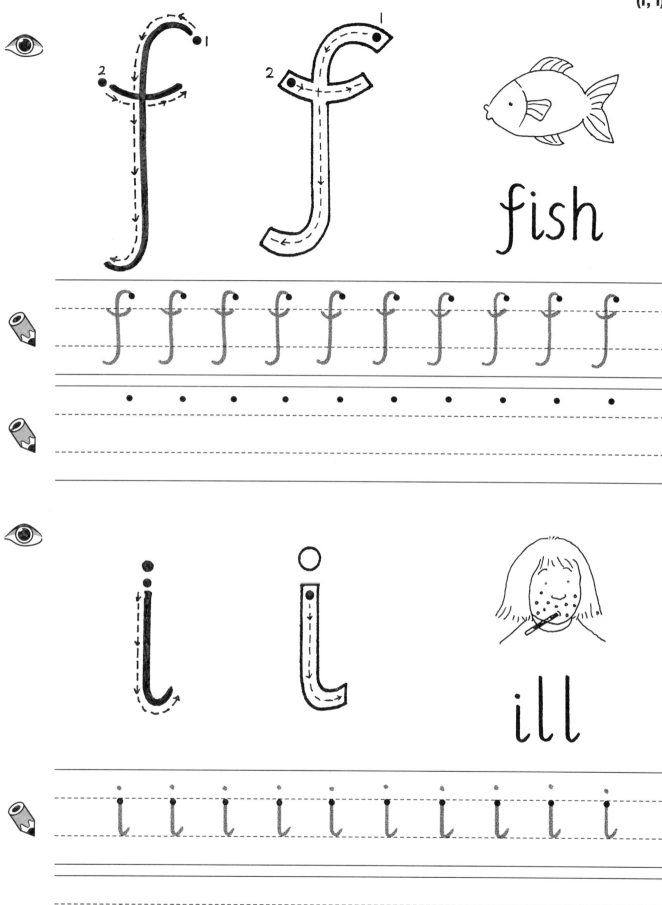

fish

ill

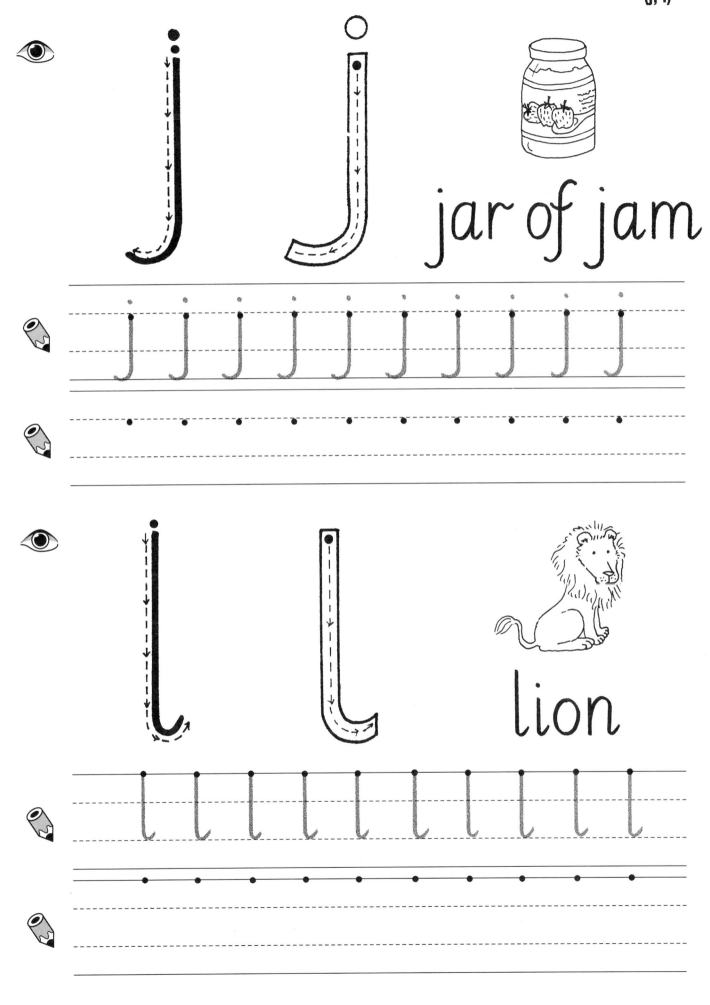

jar of jam

lion

toys

zebra

sun

umbrella

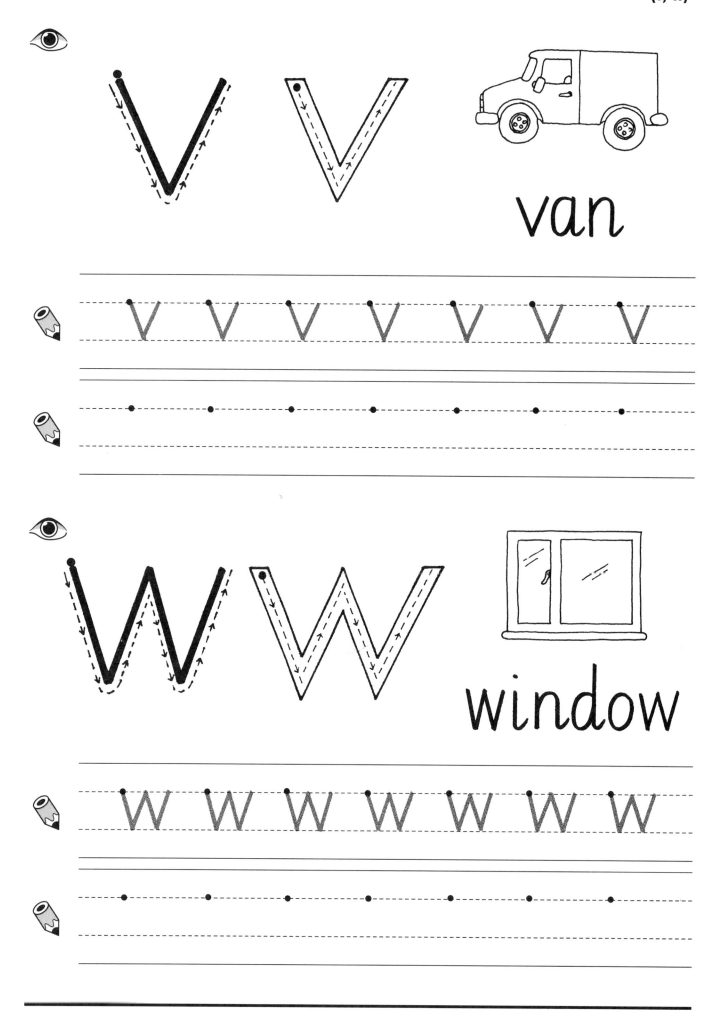

van

window

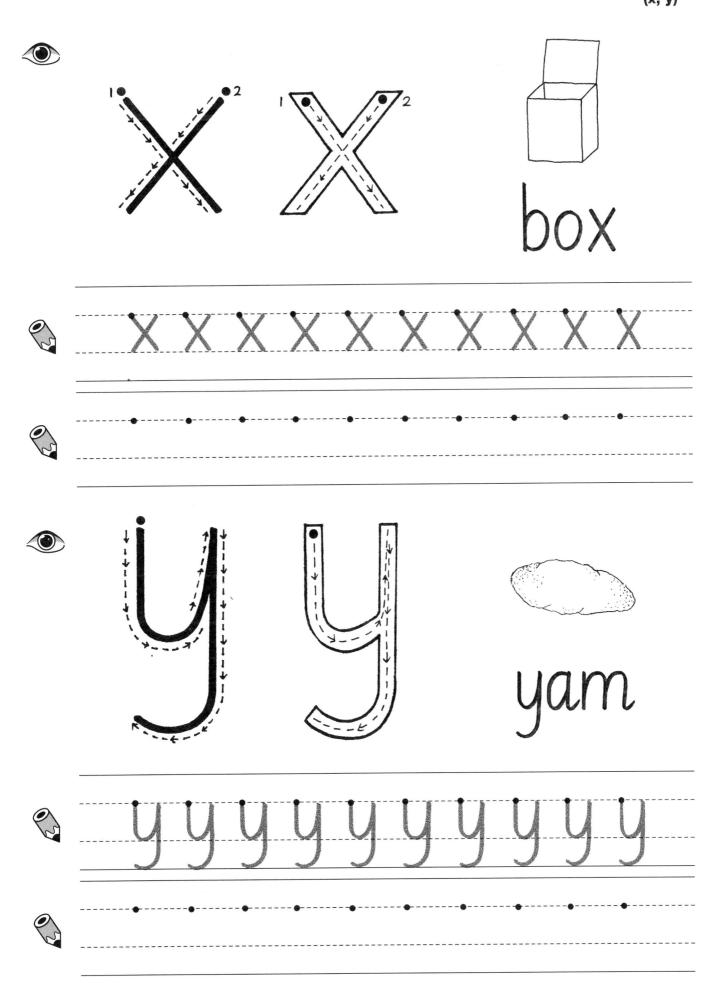

box

yam

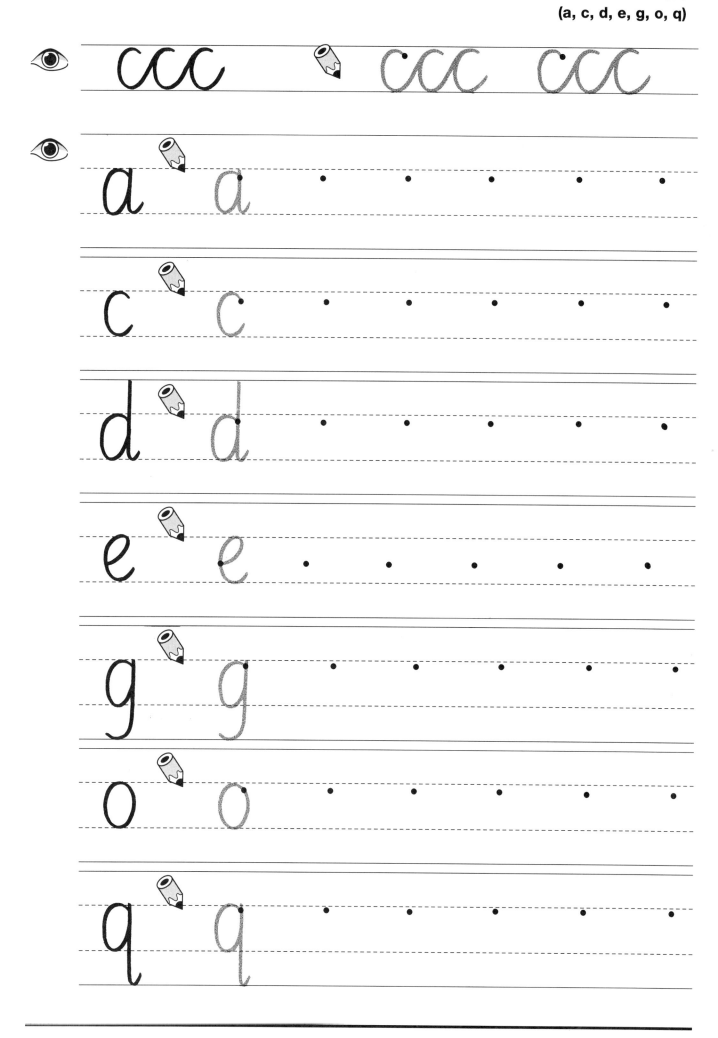

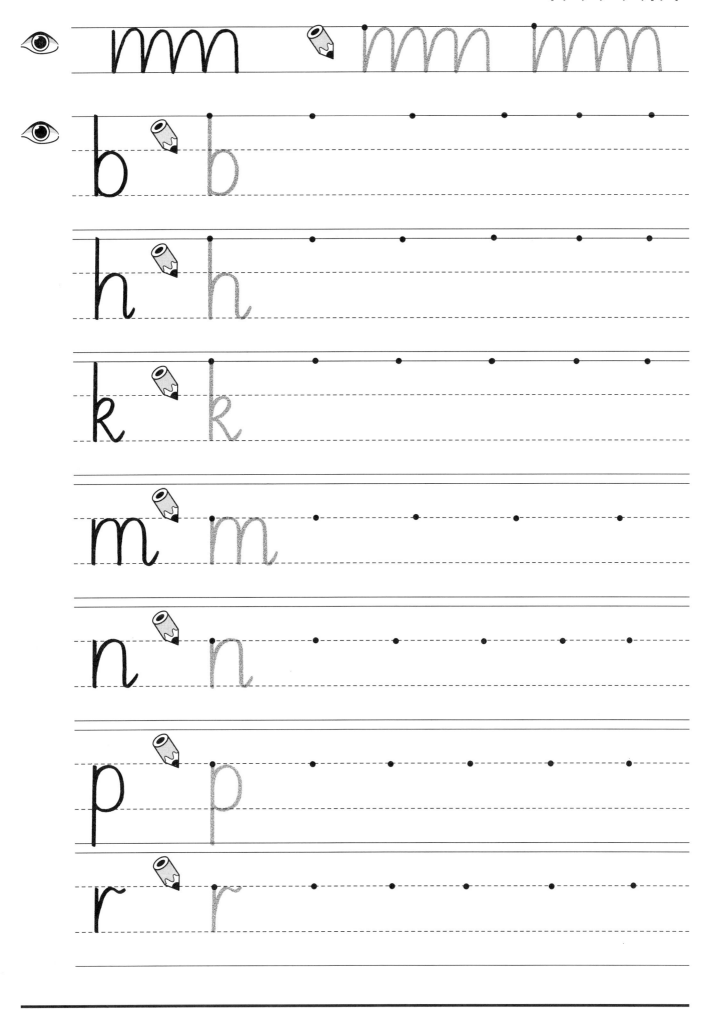

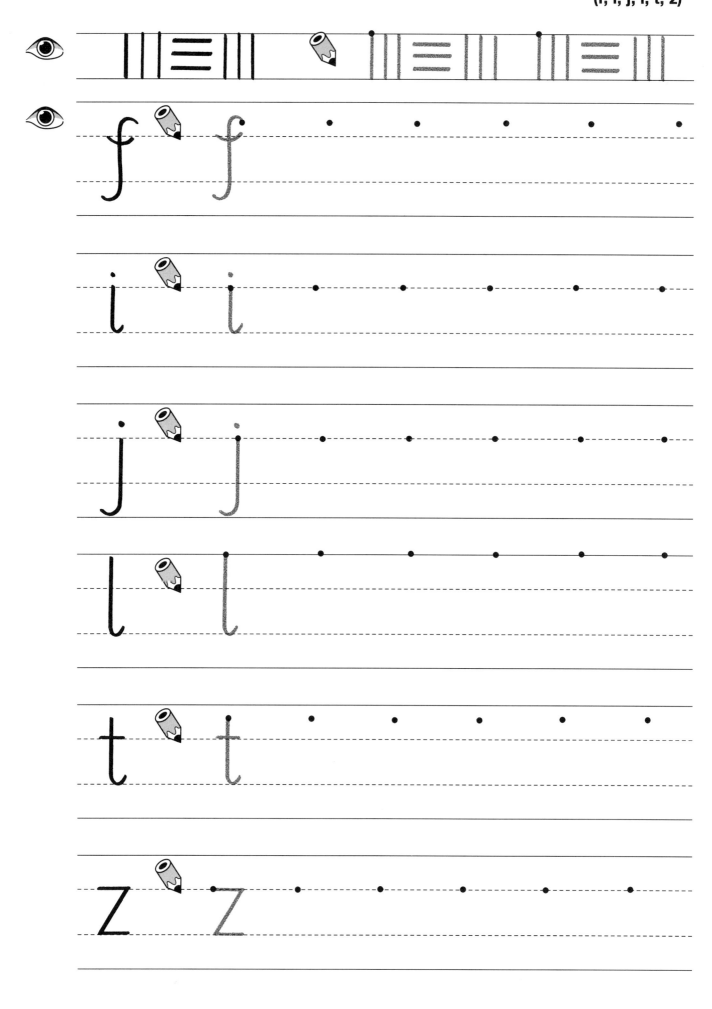

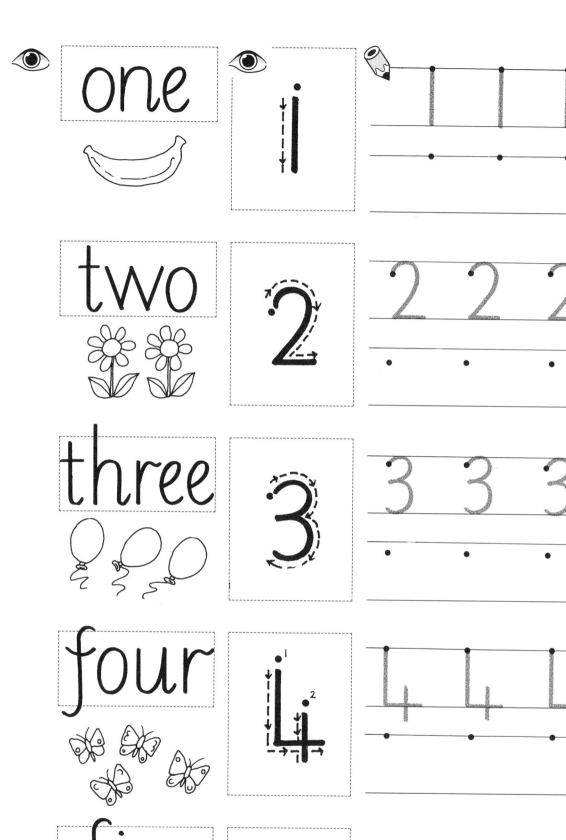

one

two

three

four

five

six

6 6 6 6

seven

7 7 7 7

eight

8 8 8 8

nine

9 9 9 9

ten

10 10 10

1, 2, buckle my shoe,

3, 4, knock at the door,

5, 6, pick up sticks,

7, 8, lay them straight,

9, 10, a big fat hen.

1 stroke; straight lines

2 strokes; straight lines

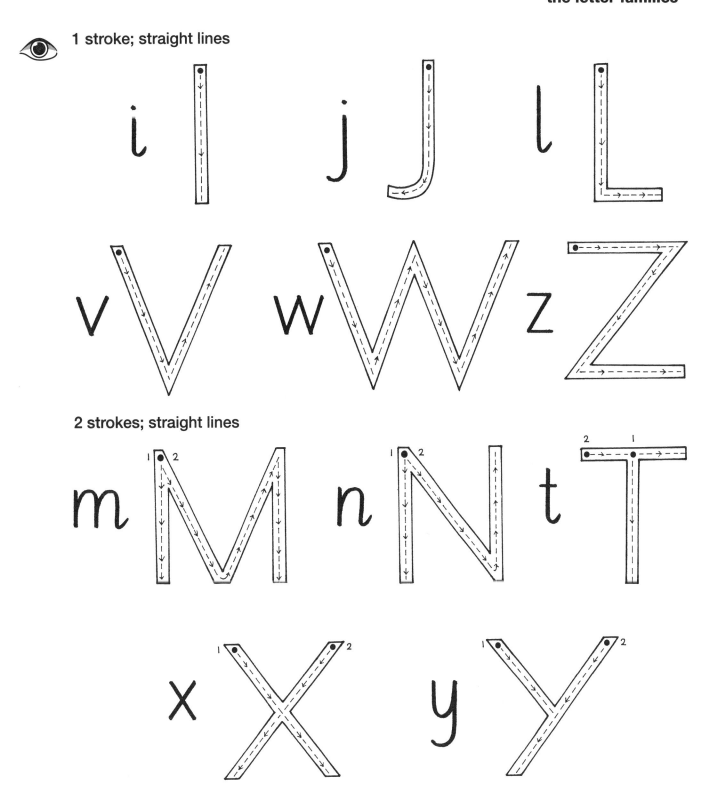

3 strokes; straight lines

1 stroke; curved lines

2 strokes; curved/straight lines

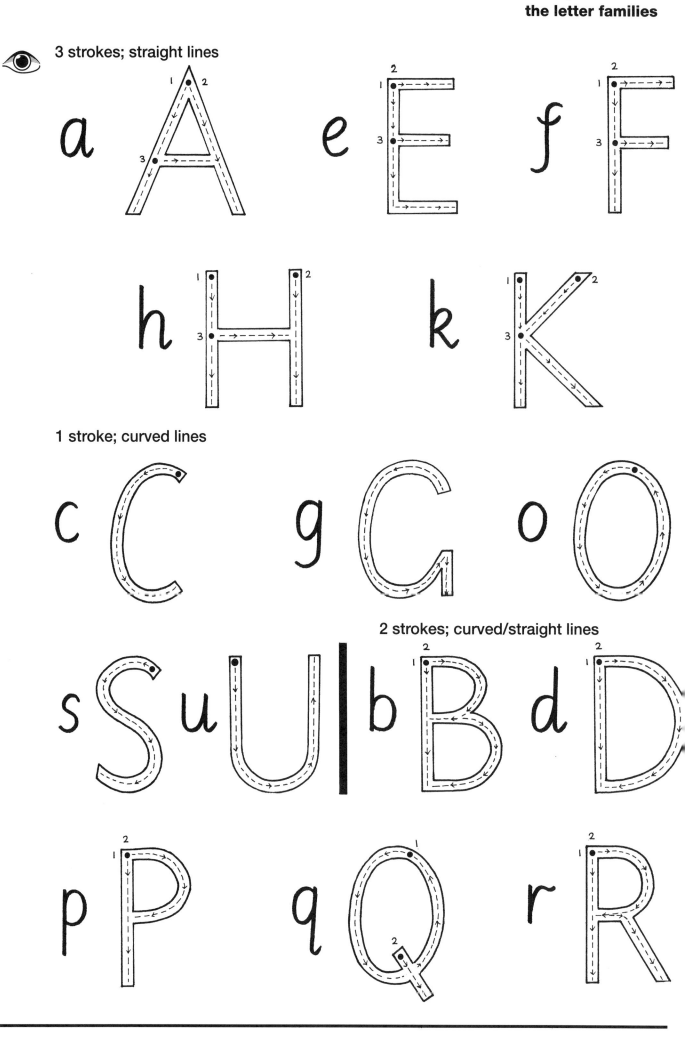

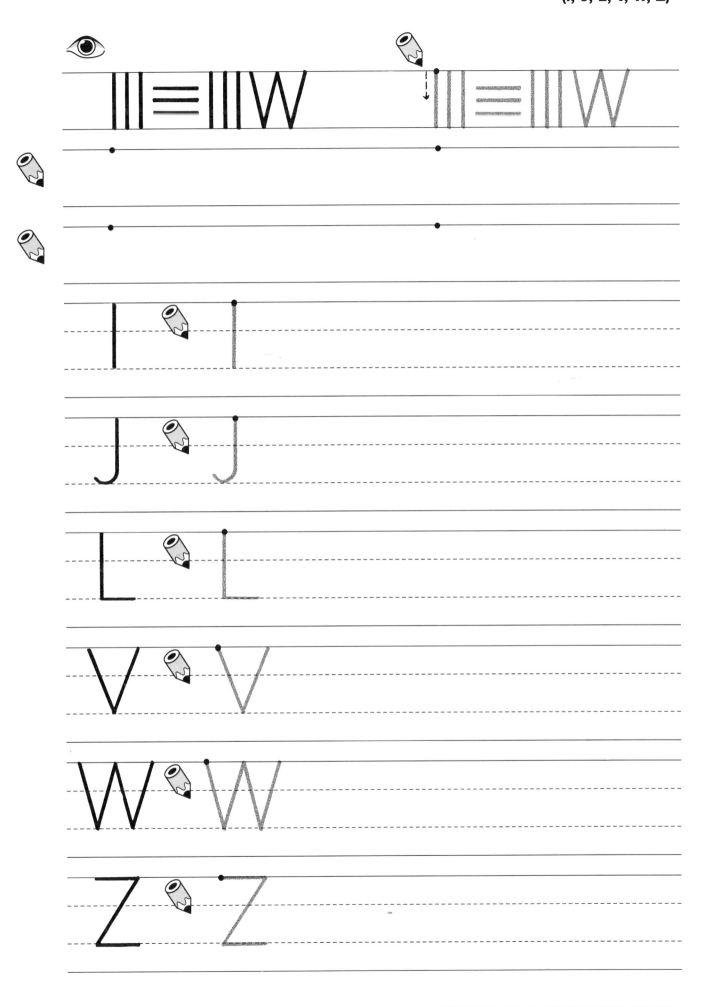

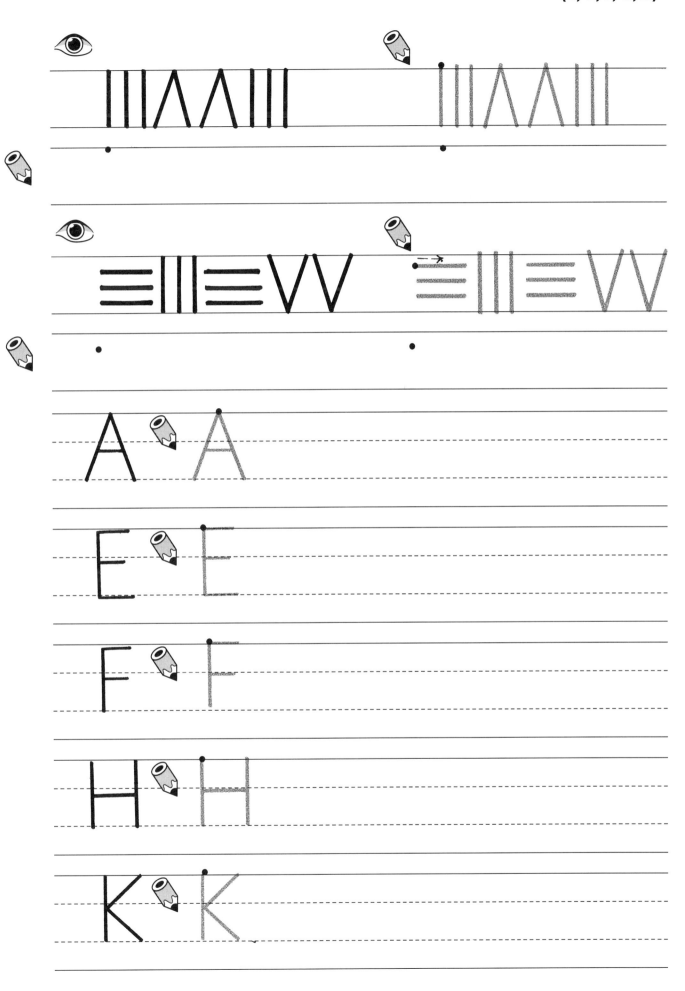

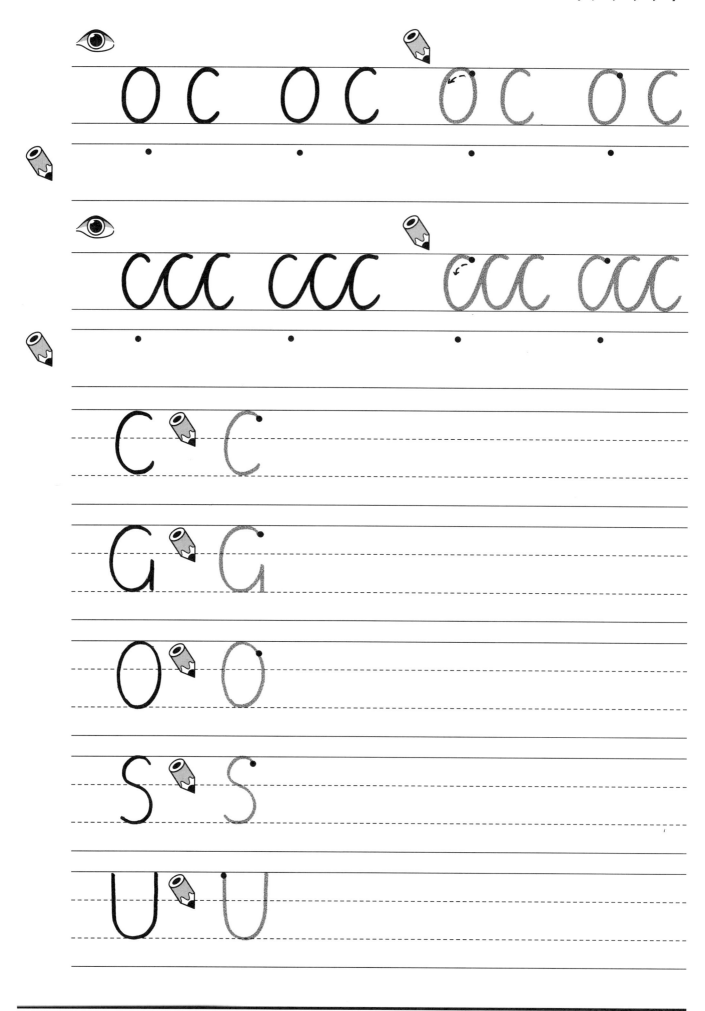

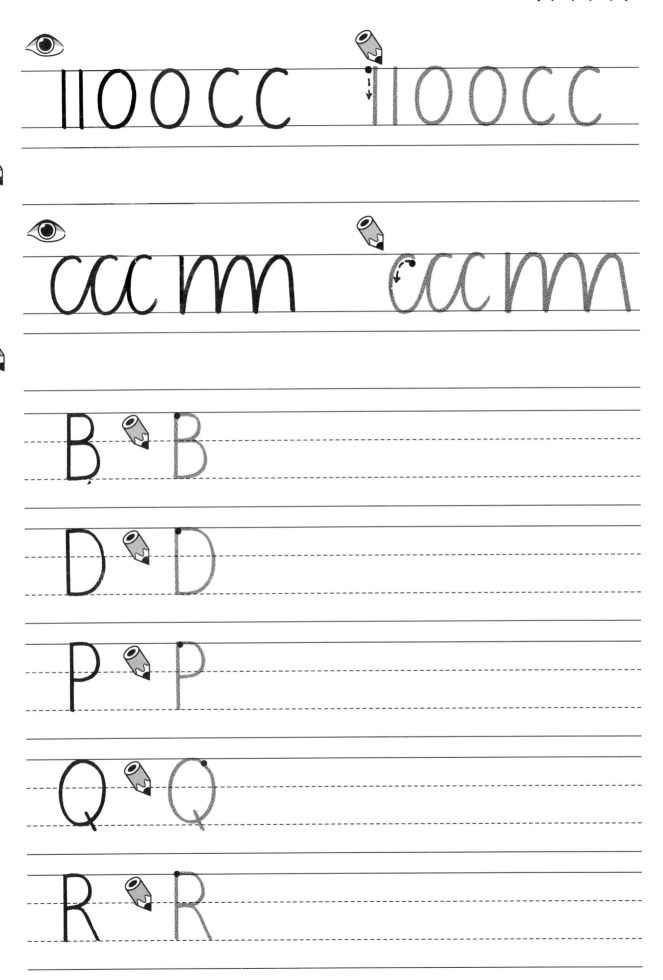

👁 A rabbit raced a turtle,
You know the turtle won;
And Mister Bunny came
in late,
A little hot cross bun!

👁 A rabbit raced a turtle,
You know the turtle won;
And Mister Bunny came
in late,
A little hot cross bun!

_in_   _im_   _iv_

_in_   _in_   _in_   _in_   _in_

_im_   _im_   _im_   _im_

_iv_   _iv_   _iv_   _iv_   _iv_

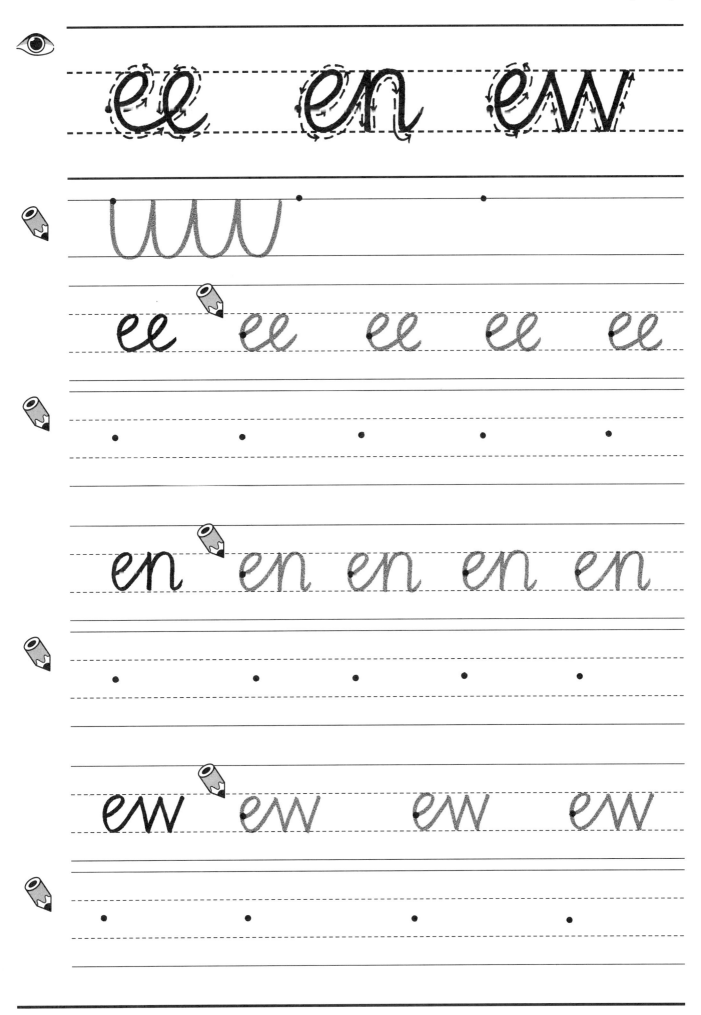

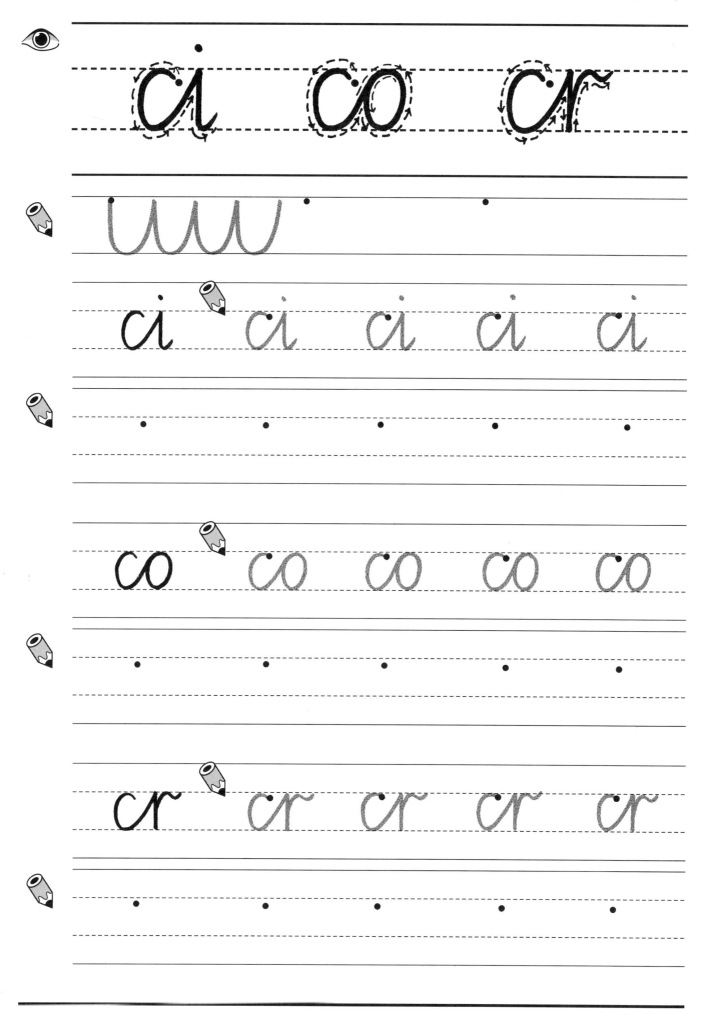

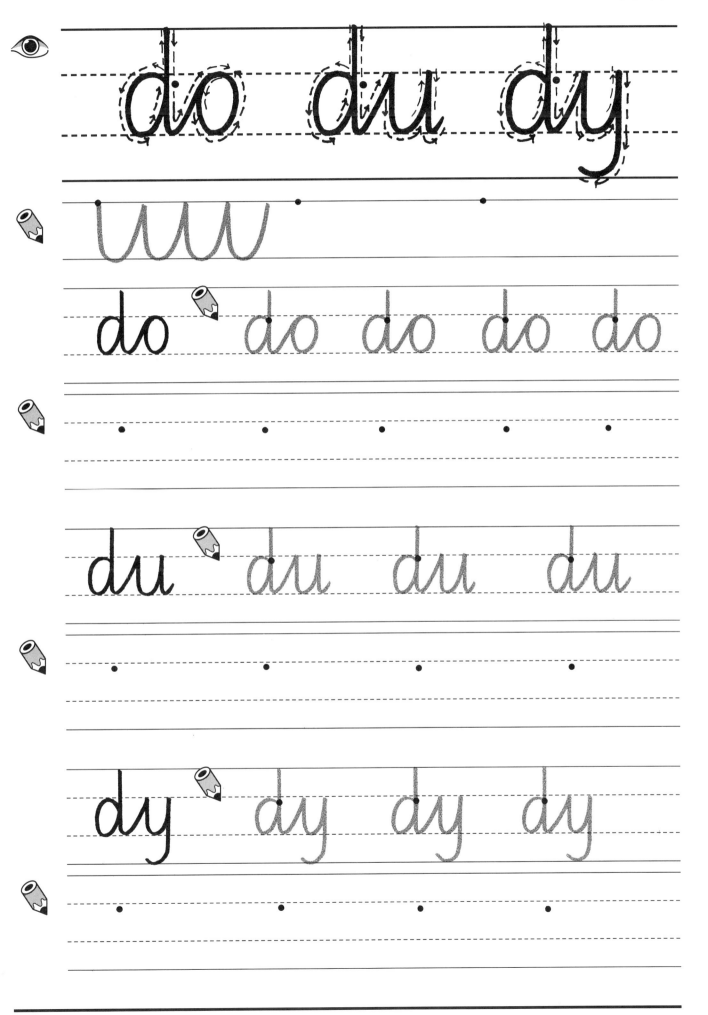

ae ai as

uuu

ae   ae   ae   ae   ae

ai   ai   ai   ai   ai

as   as   as   as   as

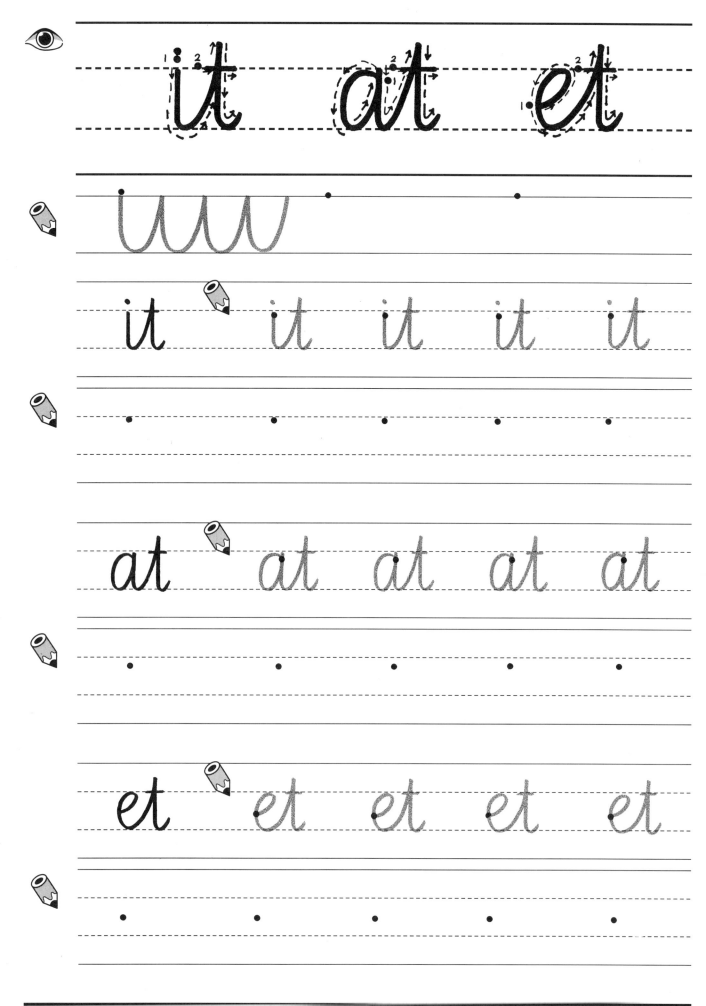